Newgrange

& Brú na Bóinne

Paul Francis

ISBN: 978-0-9926143-3-1

Published by: Charial Publishing

Ireland's Built Heritage series

Designed by: Paul Francis

All illustrations by the author, with thanks to the Office of Public Works (OPW)

Editorial Consultant: Tara Horan

Archaeological Consultant: Isabel Bennett

With special thanks to: Clare Tuffy (photos p. 20, 27, 63)

Thanks also to Aideen Gough, Pat McCusker, Maeve Francis also Paul McMahon and Tom Fitzgerald (OPW)

Photos (p. 1, 4, 19, 23, 25, 28, 31, 39, 47, 54, 55, 59, 61, 64) by kind permission of the © National Monuments Service, Dept of Arts, Heritage and the Gaeltacht. With thanks to Tony Roche

Survey drawing (p. 56) by kind permission of the O'Kelly Archive (NMS). With thanks to Ann Lynch

Designed and printed in Ireland

For additional copies e-mail: Paulfrancisdesign@gmail.com

Contents

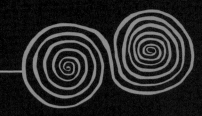

The view from the chamber of Newgrange looking down the passage towards the entrance

Newgrange rediscovered

Just over 300 years ago, a farmer named Charles Campbell, who lived close to the River Boyne in the east of Ireland, gathered his men with their picks and shovels and sent them to dig for stone from the grassy mound on the hillside above his farm, where he knew they would find all the stone that was needed.

The men set to work removing the grass sod and before long they were digging stones from the mound. As they dug, a deep hole appeared in the ground before them. Peering in, they saw great vertical stones forming a long passageway which disappeared into the hillside. One of the men crawled through, until he could stand and examine the great stones that stood before him.

Campbell joined him and they bravely pushed on further down the passageway, crawling on their knees at points, until finally squeezing through two giant stones that had come together, they found themselves standing in a large chamber, a great stone-built roof soaring above them. Even then, 300 years ago, Campbell knew that they had discovered something both ancient and extraordinary.

By coincidence a Welsh antiquarian*, Edward Lhwyd, was visiting Ireland and he made the journey to Newgrange soon after its discovery. In so doing, he became the first person in modern times to record and interpret what had been found at Newgrange, describing it as 'some place of sacrifice of the ancient Irish'. In the centuries since then, many antiquarians and early archaeologists have sought to interpret what they have found there, but only modern archaeology, aided by new scientific methods, would provide any of the answers to the many mysteries of Newgrange.

In 1962, Newgrange was purchased by the state and soon after became the site of the first large scale archaeological excavation in the nation's history. It would, in time, be revealed by the work of Professor Michael J. O'Kelly and his team to be one of the oldest, most sophisticated and beautiful buildings ever built.

Claire O'Kelly, wife of Professor O'Kelly and also an archaeologist, investigated Irish manuscripts (of the last 1,000 years) and established that, despite the collapse of its exterior and its dormant state, the fame and importance of Newgrange had lasted nearly 5,000 years until the 17th century. Three terrible wars in that century had all but eradicated the scholars and poets of Gaelic Ireland who had written of Newgrange and its place in the history and mythology of the country.

Perhaps the greatest achievement of the O'Kellys was the discovery, through careful observation and restoration, of the alignment of the passage and chamber of Newgrange with the rising sun on the morning of the winter solstice, the shortest day of the year. On the 21st of December, 1967, Professor O'Kelly, standing alone in the chamber of Newgrange, became the first person in thousands of years to witness the sun enter this ancient building, in an event which had been conceived and created more than 200 generations before.

*An antiquarian is an early archaeologist

The plough is introduced into Europe
4500BC

The wheel is invented in Mesopotamia
3500BC

4000BC

Hunter gatherers gradually move north from their refuges in Spain and southern France
13,000BC

Glaciers start to retreat
14,000BC
15,000BC

A Neolithic man, known today as 'Otzi', dies in the Italian Alps
3300BC

First Irish megalithic monuments at Carrowmore, Co. Sligo
4000BC

The Neolithic
The first farmers in Ireland start to clear forest for farmland
4200BC

12,000BC

Céide fields in Co. Mayo is the oldest known field system in the world
3500BC

11,000BC

Unification of Upper and Lower Egypt
3100BC

Newgrange, Knowth and Dowth are built in Brú na Bóinne
c. 3200BC

3000BC

10,000BC

Glaciers continue to melt. The landscape of Ireland is grassland, similar to present day Siberia

Ice Age

Giant Irish Deer roam the land

Great pyramids of Giza built in Egypt
2500BC

Bronze Age in Ireland.
Bronze axe from Newgrange

A wooden henge monument erected beside Newgrange
c. 2500BC

9000BC

Ireland becomes an island as melting glaciers raise sea level

Great sarsen stones erected at Stonehenge
c. 2400BC

Great stone circle erected around Newgrange soon after wooden henge

Vegetation in Ireland changes from grassland to deciduous forest. Large mammals, such as Giant Irish Deer, are replaced by smaller mammals such as Red Deer

8000BC

Mesolthic Age begins
People migrate by boat from Britain and are the first people in Ireland

2000BC

Gleninsheen gold collar

Iron Age in Ireland.
Hill of Tara, on the River Boyne, is seat of High King of Ireland
420BC

Great hall constructed at Navan fort and burnt soon afterwards
94BC

Moses leads the Israelites out of Egypt
c.1290BC

Greeks destroy city of Troy
c.1200BC

1000BC

Foundation of Rome
753BC

Hannibal crosses the Alps
218BC

Ireland in time

For much of the last 250,000 years Ireland has been covered in a great ice sheet, preventing both humans and wildlife from living there. The 'ice age' was at its coldest 20,000 years ago, but soon after, temperatures started to rise and the land was slowly released from the ice. In time wildlife was able to re-establish itself in Ireland.

About ten thousand years ago the first people arrived (probably from Scotland) and for the next 4,000 years, generation after generation lived a nomadic hunter-gatherer lifestyle in Mesolithic (Middle Stone Age) Ireland.

The introduction of farming about 6,000 years ago ended this nomadic way of life and brought about a new era, the Neolithic or New Stone Age. Farming and all that it brought proved to be the greatest change in the lives of Irish people in all of their 10,000 year history.

5000BC

Early farmers in the Nile Valley, Egypt
5500BC

Britain becomes separated from Continental Europe by rising seas caused by melting glaciers
c. 6000BC

6000BC

Temperatures start to rise

Last Glacial Maximum 20,000 years ago. Ice age is at its peak

Sea levels are lower than today and Ireland is connected to Britain and Continental Europe

Ireland is covered by an ice sheet 2km deep and is inhospitable to humans and wildlife

7000BC
People live by hunting and gathering close to the coast and rivers
c.7000BC

Great Cistercian Abbey of Mellifont granted lands at Brú an Bóinne and rename it 'Newgrange'
1348

Three wars in Ireland in the 17th century devastate Gaelic Ireland. Amongst the last engagements is the Battle of the Boyne, when European armies come to Brú na Bóinne to fight for the kingship of England, Ireland and Scotland
1690

Brú na Bóinne recognised by UNESCO as World Heritage site
1993

Modern excavation of Newgrange
1962–75

Newgrange, Knowth and Dowth are listed for protection as National Monuments
1882

River Boyne Canal built
1748

Newgrange rediscovered
1699

Dissolution of the Monasteries including Mellifont
1539

2000AD
The digital age begins

Otzi's body is discovered preserved in ice in the Italian Alps
1991

Medieval period
Normans invade Ireland 1169
They build their biggest castle at Trim on the Boyne
1176

Early Christian (Early Medieval) Era
St Patrick celebrates Easter by lighting a fire on the Hill of Slane, 4km from Brú na Bóinne, in defiance of the pagan King Laoghaire. Laoghaire eventually allows him to convert the Irish to Christianity
433AD

Vikings on the Boyne. Knowth and Dowth raided
820

Industrial age begins
Late 18th century

1000AD
Normans invade England
1066

The Spanish Armada is wrecked on north and west coast of Ireland
1588

0BC
Birth of Christ

End of the Western Roman Empire
476AD

Irish monks leave the island of Iona in Scotland for the monastery of Kells (on a tributary of the Boyne) to finish the Book of Kells
800

Roman Empire

The Neolithic

The introduction of farming about 6,000 years ago brought about many changes, not just in the production of food and the introduction of new artefacts, but in the way people living in Ireland viewed the land beneath their feet. Farming meant a huge investment of time and energy, firstly in changing the forest to farmable land and then in the planting and harvesting of crops. Irish people now lived permanently in the areas that they farmed, formed a bond with the land and marked it with their houses, villages and monuments.

Houses

Neolithic houses were strong, single storey, substantial, and comfortable. The walls were made from split logs and the roof, pitched high to avoid sparks from the fire, was thatched using reeds or straw. The hearth was centrally located to heat the entire house. Around the year 3000BC, the shape of houses changed from rectangular to circular or oval (right).

Villages grew in size, where specialist labour could be centred and, as a result, trade in such things as food, fur and flint tools became easier.

Stone

Flint was the most important material of the Neolithic. Such was its versatility, that it could be shaped into a heavy polished axe for tree felling or 'knapped' into a razor sharpe edge for arrow heads or delicate scrapers. There is a plentiful supply in the northern half of Ireland.

Pottery

Along with the changes in food production came other innovations such as the humble clay pot, which kept food safe from hungry animals, meaning it could be stored for leaner times. The pot also allowed food to be boiled, which turned meat and vegetables into a stew and cereals into porridge. Infants could be weaned earlier and older people with failing teeth could now keep their nutrition up, thereby extending their lives and sharing with the community their knowledge and experience.

Bread

Finding or producing food has always been the most important activity for people. Farming meant that people could now rely on food that they had stored during the good times, for hungrier times in the future.

The introduction of wheat and other crops was the greatest change to diet in the Neolithic, either as a porridge or a flat bread. It was ground on a specially shaped stone called a quern (above). The flour was stored underground or high up before being baked into bread when needed.

Hunting and gathering was still used as an efficient way of obtaining food that nature had provided.

The Neolithic = New Stone Age
In Ireland from c. 4200BC to c. 2500BC

Animals

Most of the animals chosen to be domesticated in Neolithic times are the ones still to be found on farms today. The pig provided meat when it was needed and proved to be the most farmed of all animals; up to 60% of bones found at some Neolithic sites are of pig. The other animals chosen to be farmed were the ones which proved to be the most useful. Cattle could do heavy work, provided meat and leather, and also provided renewable food in the form of milk and blood for puddings. Goats and sheep, which were introduced into Ireland, were equally valuable.

The congregation of people and animals together for the first time led to its own problems. In Neolithic Ireland only two animals posed a physical threat to humans, the bear and the wolf (both now extinct), but diseases such as flu, tuberculosis and measles were carried by newly domesticated animals and jumped to humans. In the Neolithic, life was short – 33 years on average. Surviving beyond childhood though, meant that the chances of living into your fifties was quite high.

The Megaliths of the Neolithic

At the same time as people in Ireland and Atlantic Europe were adopting the Neolithic way of life, they were also sharing a similar passage-tomb building culture. From Portugal in the south to Sweden and Denmark in the north, people were constructing passage-tombs over a span of several thousand years. They also shared technology and traded with each other over long distances by sea.

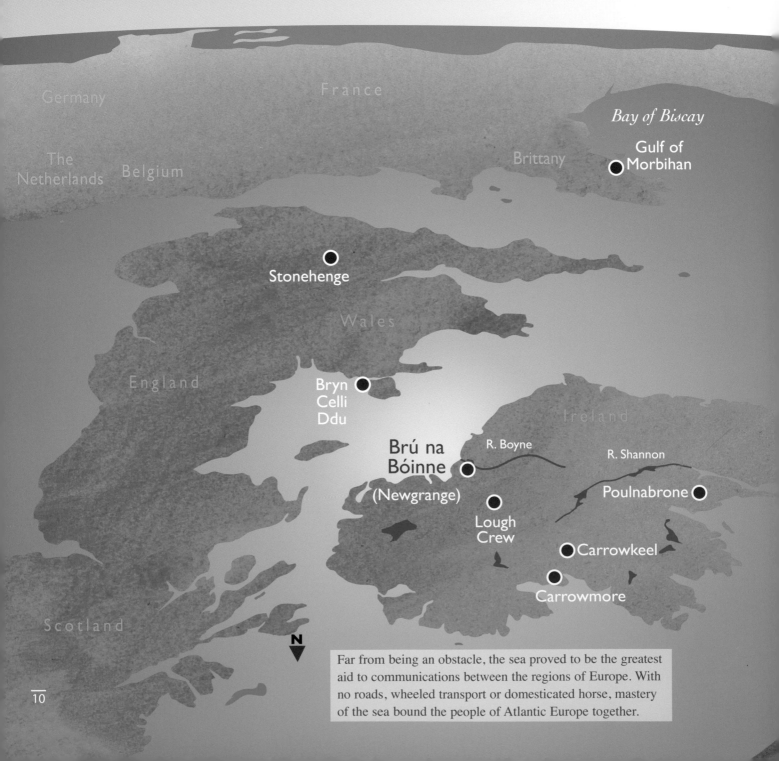

Germany

France

Bay of Biscay

The Netherlands Belgium

Brittany

Gulf of Morbihan

Stonehenge

Wales

England

Bryn Celli Ddu

Ireland

Brú na Bóinne

R. Boyne

R. Shannon

(Newgrange)

Poulnabrone

Lough Crew

Carrowkeel

Carrowmore

Scotland

N

Far from being an obstacle, the sea proved to be the greatest aid to communications between the regions of Europe. With no roads, wheeled transport or domesticated horse, mastery of the sea bound the people of Atlantic Europe together.

This time is also known as the Megalithic Age, from the Greek *mega* – great and *lithos* – stones. It was characterised by the building of monuments made of great stones of which the passage-tomb is one type. Each region had its own particular style of passage-tomb built with megaliths or great stones, but the similarities were much greater than their differences. The passage-tombs of Spain, Portugal and Brittany share the greatest similarities in design with the tombs of Brú na Bóinne. The carved art of the interior of one of Brittany's greatest tombs, Gavrinis, bears close comparison with that of some of Newgrange's carved art.

Spain

Portugal

Atlantic
Ocean

Ireland in the Megalithic Era

In the fourth millennium BC, Ireland became a major centre of megalithic tomb building. The earliest passage-tombs are found at Carrowmore, Co. Sligo. The surviving 45 smaller tombs are grouped in a cemetery with one very large tomb at its centre. Later cemeteries are found at Carrowkeel, Co. Sligo and Lough Crew (50km from Brú na Bóinne). Isolated tombs were also built at this time, as well as other variations on the passage-tomb known as court tombs, wedge tombs and portal dolmens (below).

Monuments such as the portal dolmen at Poulnabrone, Co. Clare, (right) were probably built in the early fourth millennium BC

Brú na Bóinne

The River Boyne is one of the great rivers of Ireland. It flows from the central plain of Ireland for 112km and reaches the Irish Sea at the medieval town of Drogheda. From the earliest times, the Boyne has been used as an important highway into the heartland of Ireland, as well as being a rich provider of much of what was needed for people to survive in Neolithic times.

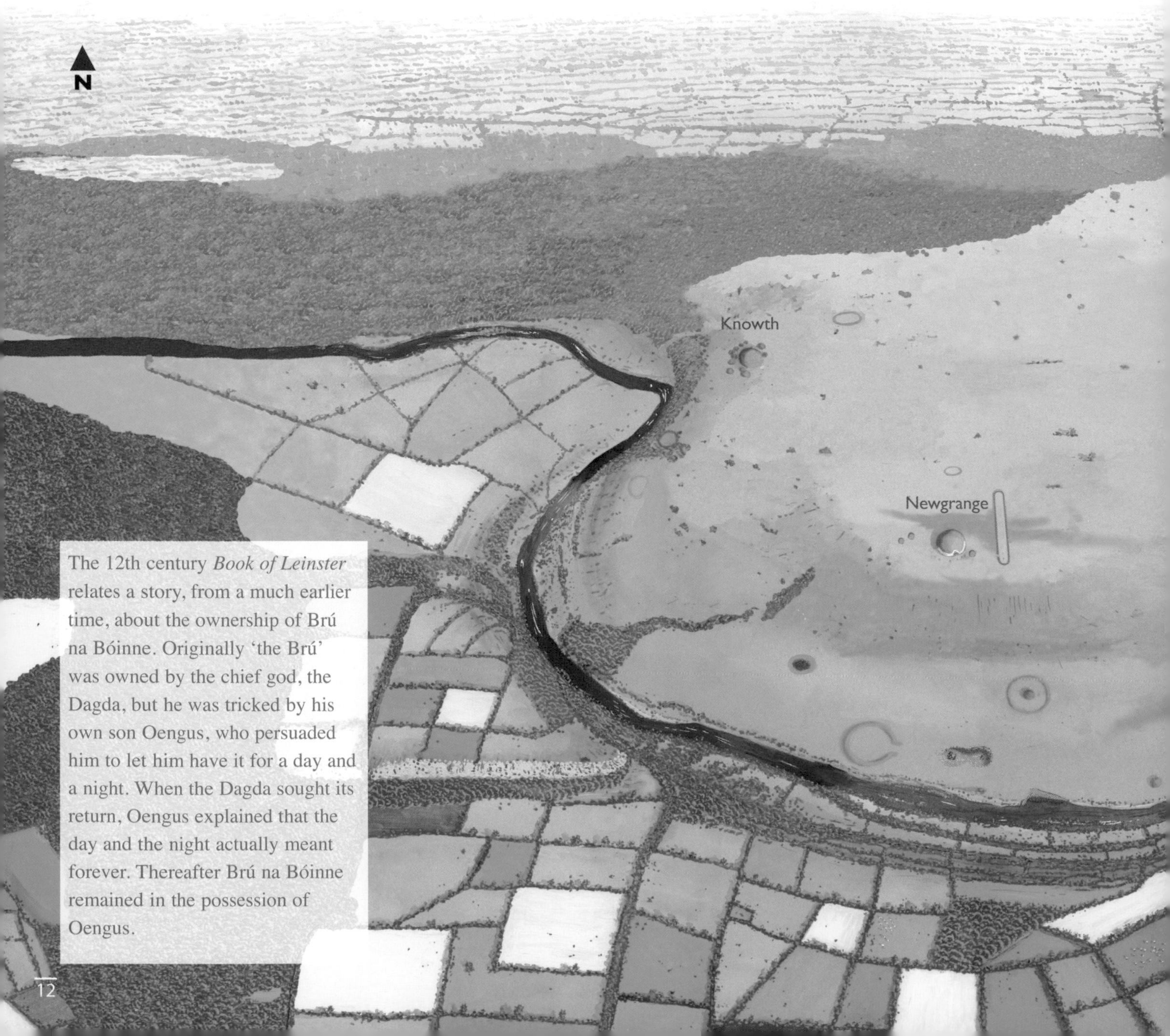

N

Knowth

Newgrange

The 12th century *Book of Leinster* relates a story, from a much earlier time, about the ownership of Brú na Bóinne. Originally 'the Brú' was owned by the chief god, the Dagda, but he was tricked by his own son Oengus, who persuaded him to let him have it for a day and a night. When the Dagda sought its return, Oengus explained that the day and the night actually meant forever. Thereafter Brú na Bóinne remained in the possession of Oengus.

About 16 kilometres before the River Boyne reaches the sea, it encounters high ground and is forced to turn sharply to the south. It slowly returns to its original course in a great bend or curve. Another smaller river, the Mattock, joins the Boyne at the end of this bend, creating what is almost an island. This is *Brú na Bóinne* or in English, the mansion of the Boyne.

Perhaps because rivers were considered to be deities – the Boyne was Boann, wife of the chief god, the Dagda – or perhaps because of its island-like status, or the high ground encompassed there, Neolithic people chose Brú na Bóinne to be special, a place apart. They cleared the forest and created a sacred landscape in which they built their temples and tombs, the scale and sophistication of which had never before been seen anywhere in the ancient world.

Dowth

Very little is known about the Neolithic people of the Boyne Valley, the people who built Newgrange. What they called themselves, what they looked like, how they organised their society, who their heroes and villains were, even where they lived, are some of the questions that have yet to be answered and may never be.

Just why this community of farmers agreed to start building Newgrange (and Knowth and Dowth) is perhaps the greatest question of all, for it was a commitment without parallel in Irish history. The work would engage all of them and all of their spare time for decades to come. Children not yet born would, in time, become involved in the relentless work of construction, while others who

An Irish passage-tomb of the Neolithic (including Newgrange, Knowth and Dowth) contains several common features regardless of its size:

▮ A passage leading to a chamber. The passage can vary greatly in length and height, but can always accommodate a fully grown person

▮ A chamber. Chambers vary in size, shape and height. Recesses are also a common feature, often in a cruciform (cross-shaped) plan

▮ A kerb made of large stones, which defines the shape and size of the passage-tomb

▮ A cairn, also know as a tumulus or mound. It was usually made of small stones, but in larger passage-tombs could be constructed using soil and turves in alternate layers

▮ A basin stone is sometimes found in the chamber or the recesses. It was used as a receptacle for cremated remains and grave goods

▮ Passage-tombs are often sited on high ground. Newgrange, Knowth and Dowth are sited on the three highest points in Brú na Bóinne

▮ Passage-tombs are most often grouped together in cemeteries, where small satellite tombs surround larger tombs.

started to build, would not live to see Newgrange completed. The need for a place to honour those who had died in the community, together with a burning religious energy, must have provided the inspiration for their plans.

The overall design, a passage-tomb (below), was an obvious choice, since there were smaller passage-tombs already built in Brú na Bóinne. Scaling it up over 100 times and overcoming the technical difficulties which that brought was an unprecedented challenge. They cannot have known whether some parts of the building, such as the roof, were even possible.

The greatest challenge though, was not to start building, but to keep going after the initial enthusiasm of people had waned and see it through to its completion.

Later ancient peoples referred to the Neolithic people of Ireland as the Tuatha Dé Danann. They believed them to be supernatural beings, who belonged to a remote past, but continued to live underground in the mounds and cairns that they had built, occasionally venturing forth into the world of people.

Cut-away of a passage-tomb

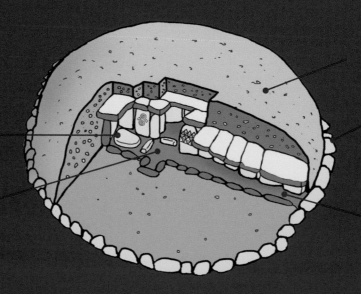

Basin stone

Chamber
(with 3 recesses)

Cairn, tumulus or mound

Kerbstones

Passage

First light of the winter solstice

At some point before work began on construction, an idea came to the fore. What if, on the morning of the shortest day of the year, the winter solstice, the first rays of sunlight could enter the chamber of Newgrange for a short time, in a union between the sun and the earth! This would make Newgrange more than just a building, but a living structure that interacted and communed with the sun, the probable god of the people.

To achieve this, the builders would have to establish precisely where the sun rose on the other side of the valley on that morning and align it with both where the front of the passage and the back of the chamber would be. They would then build the whole structure around these points of alignment.

In order for the alignment to work successfully, it was important that no other light should enter the chamber at any other time, except for a direct beam from the sun on the winter solstice. Great care would be needed to establish the length and shape of the passage. The chamber needed to be as dark as possible all year round and yet allow light to enter only for that short time.

Having established this important alignment, construction could begin around it. Once begun, the people of the Boyne Valley now had to commit to years of relentless hard work, most of it pulling, shoving and lifting. A smaller group would direct the construction and an even smaller group of artists would carve designs on the stones.

Ancient astronomers

A knowledge of astronomy and the movement of the sun, moon and stars across the sky would have allowed the people of the Boyne Valley to measure time and predict the seasons. How much more they knew, has yet to be properly established, but the star-filled skies of ancient Ireland (unhindered by modern light) must have inspired some sort of understanding of their place in time and space.

Horizon line

(above) In order to create and maintain an alignment with the rising sun of the winter solstice and the proposed passage and chamber (which would take many years to build), a series of aligned posts with apertures may have been used

The winter and summer solstice

(solstice, from Latin solstitium, from sol 'sun' and stit 'stopped')

Every day of the year the sun rises in a slightly different place on the horizon (below). In the summer, the arc that the sun travels through in the sky is high and wide, but every day after the 21st June (summer solstice) the arc slowly declines all the way to the 21st December, the winter solstice, when the sun is at its lowest arc in the sky. The sun 'stops' its decline on this morning and is 'reborn'. Thereafter the arc of the sun will be higher and wider as the sunrise returns back to the east.

Summer solstice – arc of the sun

Equinox

Winter solstice

South

East

West

Sunrise

Sunset

Building materials

The materials used to build Newgrange tell us a great deal about its builders and their attention to detail. Where a particular type of stone was needed, they went to great efforts to locate it and then transport it, often as much as 60km.

Newgrange is constructed from six main types of material:

- **Small loose stones** (right) make up the greatest amount of material of the cairn of Newgrange. This enormous amount of stone (200,000 tonnes) was collected from sites close to the River Boyne. A small lake, which today is 750 metres from Newgrange, is the probable stone quarry. The average size of these stones is about 22cm x 15cm

- **Turves** were used in the cairn to prevent the loose stones from slipping outwards. A turve is the first layer of soil and grass combined and is about 10cm thick and can be several metres long. A large mound of turves was also built within the cairn (see p.25)

- The **great stones** of Newgrange. There are over 550 great stones found at Newgrange, each weighing between one and 10 tonnes (a medium sized car weighs about 1.5 tonnes), from which the kerb, passage and chamber were built. Many of these stones were unearthed and collected from the surrounding countryside. We know this because their surfaces

display signs of weathering. Other great stones may have been quarried and borne by boat on the River Boyne to below the site, where they had to be heaved uphill for 1km. All but two of these stones are a hard slate known as greywacke

- The white mineral **Quartz** is found mostly on the southern side of the cairn where it forms a facade (left). It was brought from the Wicklow mountains over 60km to the south

- **Water-rolled granite boulders**. These rocks were collected from the shore of Dundalk Bay, 35km north of Newgrange. They were used in the facade of Newgrange (left)

- **Waterproofing material**. A mixture of burnt soil and sand, which has a putty-like consistency was used to seal and waterproof between the stones of the roof. Other than that, no mortar was used in the building of Newgrange.

Newgrange
61m above sea level

750m

River Boyne
5m above sea level

| Quarry

If only one person had to build Newgrange!

The cairn of Newgrange contains an estimated 200,000,000 kilos of material, most of which was quarried from the floodplain of the River Boyne, 750 metres below the monument. The figure-of-eight shaped quarry is now a small lake.

One person carrying 20 kilos of stone (about the weight of two average car tyres) could make 15 return journeys (1.5km x15) per day, a total of 300 kilos of stone a day.

Working every day of the year, it would take one person 1,826 years just to build the cairn.

If 500 people were available to work every day, it would take three and a half years, although more effective methods could be employed with more people involved.

(above) The largest visible stone at Newgrange. It measures 4m x 2m and weighs over 10 tonnes. It was used as the third roof stone in the passage. Cut into its top surface are grooves to allow water percolating through the cairn to drain away from the passage

Moving the stones

Work on the construction of Newgrange might have been much easier had the builders had a wheel. Unfortunately the wheel had only just been invented in Egypt and the horse, essential to later peoples in Europe, had not yet been domesticated. Boats, using the River Boyne, would have provided the most efficient mode of transport for both material and people.

Amongst the first stones in place were the large ceremonial basin stones. There are two in the right recess (pictured below) and one in each of the other two recesses. Their great weight and size meant that they had to be shaped, carved and put in position before the walls of the chamber were completed

First stones

Once the great stones were on site, the work changed from heaving and hauling to a more precise lifting and placing. The orthostats (upright stones) of the passage and chamber were placed in trenches as deep as 0.8m and back-filled with stones for support.

Great care was taken in choosing the orthostats for their solidity and strength. Most of the weight of the roof and the mound above it, would be placed upon the 17 stones of the chamber. If one failed then the whole structure would collapse.

The passage and chamber are 24 metres in length and the floor rises 1.6m over that distance, following the slope of the hill. A person standing at the entrance looking up the passage would be looking at the feet of a person standing in the chamber. This variation in height works to almost completely block out direct sunlight from the chamber.

Chamber

Slope of hill

Passage

A spring rises on the cairn side of this orthostat and flows away from the passage. The spring may have had some religious importance and may have influenced the exact location of Newgrange.

At this point a dry stone wall was used, instead of an orthostat, to fill this space. The purpose of the wall is unknown.

The passage is not straight. Slight curves have been built in to prevent any daylight penetrating all the way to the chamber

The Kerb

The kerb contains a total of 97 giant stones and is 270 metres in circumference. It forms the boundary and defines the shape of Newgrange, which occupies half a hectare. All the stones of the kerb were probably put in place at an early stage, thereby marking out the boundary of the monument itself and setting out the task for future generations of builders.

All the stones of the kerb appear to be the same height. They have been carefully aligned at the top to achieve a horizontal line by digging deeper holes for bigger stones. Their lengths vary greatly from 1.5m to 4.5m. The biggest is K12 (right) which is situated close to the entrance and weighs c.7 tonnes.

Many of the kerbstones are decorated, which is a feature unique to Ireland, but only three are richly decorated – K1 (the entrance stone), K52 and K67.

Built to last

The next stage was one of the most difficult and dangerous building feats of the ancient world – the construction of the chamber roof. The decision to build a stone roof over 6 metres high, which spanned a distance of 8 metres by 15 metres, was the boldest in all of Neolithic architecture. A simple low roof using great stones to span the distance would have meant less risk, but would have produced a much smaller chamber area. The ambition of the builders demanded space, height and, above all, strength, so that the chamber and its roof would last for all time.

The construction of the chamber roof involved dragging flat stones upwards into a series of steps, in a style known as corbelling, much like a stairs ascends to the next level of a house. These stones supported each other and were fixed in position without the use of mortar. Once the capstone was in place, the builders must have breathed a collective sigh of relief. Despite being of enormous weight, the capstone kept every stone below it in position.

The successful completion of the roof meant that the builders had constructed a stone chamber (or room) that has lasted longer than any other in history.

The builders realised that where the roof meets the void of the passageway there was a weak point.

To compensate for this and to avoid future collapse, this side of the chamber roof was started further down the passage, thereby spreading the load over a greater area. A relieving arch at this point, supported by stones of the cairn, also helped to support the colossal weight above the roof.

Once the chamber was complete, Newgrange may have been put to use immediately. The massive cairn would take decades more to complete and the chamber with its corbelled roof was a complete building in itself.

The chamber must have been designed to facilitate ceremonies. A high roof, three separate recesses and a large floor space, which can accommodate more than 20 people, would easily allow enough space for religious rituals to be performed.

The chamber, as well as being dry, maintains a constant temperature of 10° when the entrance is sealed.

Waterproofing

Channels (c. 30mm wide) were cut into the roof stones of the passage and probably also the chamber. Rainwater falling through the mound would be directed down through these channels and away from the chamber and passage.

A mixture of sea sand and burnt soil, which has a putty-like consistency, was applied to any spaces between the roof stones to ensure no gaps would allow water to enter. It was this substance which allowed archaeologists to accurately carbon date Newgrange at the time of the modern excavation.

The roof-box (see p.24)

The roof-box

A bove the entrance of the passage at Newgrange is a small, specially-constructed opening or aperture, known today as the roof-box.

The roof-box is a unique structure and is found nowhere else in the megalithic world. It is positioned so that when the sun rises, on the morning of the winter solstice (21st December), direct sunlight shines through its narrow aperture, travels the length of the passage and illuminates the chamber of Newgrange.

This phenomenon probably worked for many hundreds of years in the Neolithic, until, at some point in ancient times, the smaller stones (A – below) supporting the roof slab above the aperture subsided under the weight of the cairn. This led to a closing of the aperture and an end to the winter solstice phenomenon, until its rediscovery in 1967 (see p.62). The collapse of the facade of Newgrange and the burial of its entrance in the early Bronze Age, completed its demise.

(above) The roof-box today

The roof-box structure

(left) The roof-box structure was built on top of the first roof stone (R1). It served to protect the aperture from the weight of the cairn above and to block indirect sunlight.

The narrow aperture created in the gap between the giant first roof stone and the next roof stone is only 0.25m high x 1 metre wide

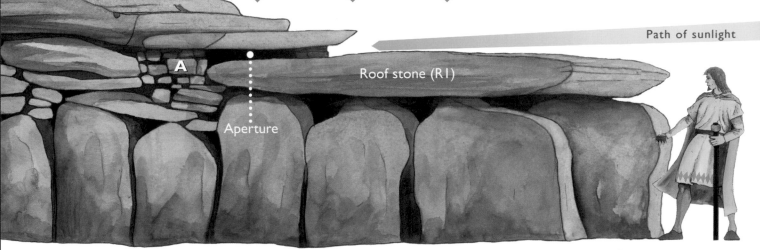

A

Aperture

Roof stone (R1)

Path of sunlight

Passage entrance

Newgrange North

On the north side of Newgrange, directly opposite the entrance, stands a magnificently carved kerbstone, known as K52 (below). The builders decided that this point of the monument was in some way important and marked it with the second most elaborately carved stone at Newgrange. This kerbstone has a distinctive dividing line running from top to bottom, which is also found on the entrance stone at the front of Newgrange and the entrance stones of the two passages at Knowth. Despite this, there appears to be no passage entrance directly behind K52.

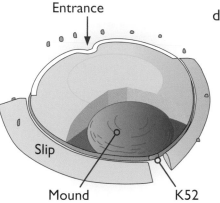

Diagram of Newgrange from the North (cut-away view) showing the position of the mound

However, there is a mound constructed entirely of turves buried under the stone cairn of Newgrange and behind K52. The mound is over 35 metres in diameter and was probably built close to the time Newgrange itself was constructed. There may therefore be a passage and chamber located somewhere within this mound. It was about 4.2 metres high when first constructed, but compacted to 1.5 metres under the weight of the cairn stones added later.

The mound was discovered as a result of the modern excavation of the 1960s, when archaeologists dug behind K52. When the mound was revealed, the grass and plants of the turves were found to be still green, over 5,000 years after they were cut from the gound.

(above) There are 42 layers of turves in the mound, which are evident in this stratified profile

(left) K52

The art of Brú na Bóinne

As work proceeded on the building of Newgrange, a small group of artists was engaged in the task of carving designs on many of the most prominent stones. Stone tools made of flint – stone on stone – were used to carve the stone. However difficult this task must have been, it did not limit the ambition of the artists. In sheer numbers of carvings alone, there is more carved art in Brú na Bóinne than in the whole of Western Europe combined (600 stones). This type of carved art in Ireland is only found in association with passage-tombs.

The amount of carving in Brú na Bóinne is matched by the huge range of symbols used by the artists; spirals, lozenges, zig-zags and circles. Applied alone or together, each design is always slightly different from the next. Long before modern art used the medium of abstraction, the artists of Brú na Bóinne had adopted it as the principal form of conveying some now lost meaning.

Many of these symbols appear again and again, sometimes appearing as substantial carvings, such as on the entrance stone to Newgrange (below) or at other times as a small, seemingly insignificant doodle.

In some instances the carvings continue under surfaces which are hidden and inaccessible, proving that the carving was done before or at the time of construction and was an integral part of the building, rather than a decorative afterthought.

The triple spiral

If there is one symbol that dominates more than any other in the art of Newgrange, it is the triple spiral (right and below left). This motif only occurs in Ireland and then only at Newgrange, despite the huge array of designs at Knowth and Dowth.

The artists of Newgrange created a symbol which seemed to communicate all that they needed to say, as it is found in two of the most important places in the tomb, on the entrance stone and in the back recess of the chamber. Its meaning has been lost to us today, but it is not unreasonable to suggest that the spiral may in someway represent the religious beliefs of the people of Brú na Bóinne. It is unlikely that we will ever know what they truly meant to convey in this carving, or indeed if it was ever meant to say anything at all. Part of the beauty of the triple spiral is its mystery.

(above) The triple spiral carving in the north recess of the chamber at Newgrange. Although this carving is commonly known as the triple spiral or tri-spiral, it actually is made up of six spirals which wind around and connect with each other on a never ending journey

The entrance stone

The entrance stone at Newgrange (left and p.64) is amongst the greatest pieces of art of the Neolithic. The stone is carved on one entire side and it faces towards the River Boyne and the rising sun on the morning of the winter solstice. It seems to form a physical and spiritual barrier between the dark world of the interior of Newgrange and the sunlit world outside of the living.

It is a combination of spiral and lozenge shapes, which are the two most prolific motifs in the Neolithic art of Brú na Bóinne. We can only guess at its meaning. Perhaps it is the face of one of their possible gods, the sun, rising above the river Boyne, which seems to swirl below or perhaps it represents the three great tombs of Newgrange, Knowth and Dowth.

Another important motif is the dividing line in the centre, which seems to split the stone into two parts. This dividing line is found on other important carved stones in Brú na Bóinne such as K52 on the north side of Newgrange (p.25) and the two entrance stones at Knowth.

The entrance stone was carved after it was placed in its current position as carving only extends as far as the old Neolithic ground level.

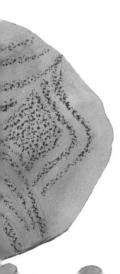

Position of L19 in passage

Orthostat L19 (above) is located in the passage. Spirals, chevrons and a single lozenge combine to make this one of Newgrange's most distinctive carving. Located on a curve close to the chamber, it seems to scream a warning to unwelcome visitors

There are 75 decorated stones at Newgrange and over 600 decorated stones in Brú na Bóinne. The motifs of the carvings fit into two main categories:

Curvilinear

circles

arcs

spirals

serpentine forms

dot in a circle

Rectilinear

chevrons

radials

lozenges

parallel lines

offsets/comb shapes

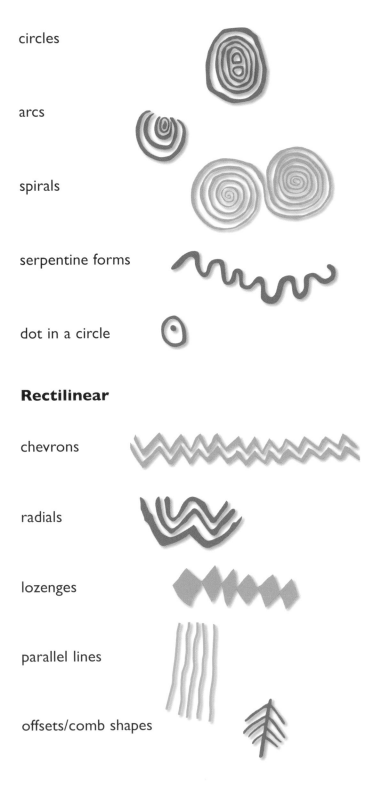

Building the cairn

The successful completion of the chamber roof meant it was the tallest (6 metres) free-standing stone building in the world. Its successful construction must have helped in the impetus for the next phase, the building of the cairn, which would require 200,000 tonnes of material to fill the area within the kerb. It seems to have been built in three different phases with gaps of several years between them (evident from the build up of soil and vegetation in the gap years).

When the roof was completed a 'boulder cap' was constructed around the chamber. The cap consisted of a layer of large round stones (c. 30cm in diameter), which completely covered the entire chamber except for the top capstone. It is believed that the boulder cap kept the angled stones of the roof in place.

The building of the cairn would take decades and such was the need for labour that work may have been centred around religious festivals, such as the winter and summer solstice, when large numbers of people, from other regions, may have visited and contributed to its construction.

Most of the material in the cairn is loose stone. A low wall of large boulders was built here on the original ground level to keep the loose stones of the cairn in place. Several layers of turves were then placed in front of the wall to provide additional support.

The cairn was faced with a facade of white quartz and granite rolled boulders (see p.58)

Turves

To add stability to the enormous amount of loose stone in the cairn, several continuous seams of turves were added.

Turves are the top layer of soil, which includes the grass and its roots to a depth of about 10cm. They were cut close to the river and transported uphill to the mound. Each seam has as many as 12 layers of turves. Over time the overall thickness was reduced due to compression.

These seams also prove that Newgrange was planned and built as a complete building. Had Newgrange been extended outwards at a later time it would have been evident in these seams, which form a continuous unbroken layer from the quartz wall deep into the cairn.

Three separate strata of turves were employed to keep the loose stones of the cairn in place. They are thickest near the facade of the cairn.

Newgrange complete

When Newgrange was completed it was one of the greatest buildings in the world, rivalled only by its near neighbour Knowth (p.46), 1 kilometre away. It stood over 13 metres high and was 85 metres in diameter. No structure outside of Brú na Bóinne could compare to its size, complexity and the quality of its art, both inside and out. In the Neolithic landscape of green forest and fields, the gleaming white quartz facade was a beacon and a statement of the spiritual energy of the people of the Boyne Valley.

Two small features near the entrance completed the architectural complex of Newgrange: an open-ended (towards Newgrange) hut stood a few metres to the southwest of the entrance and a small oval setting made of flag stones and cobbles, was built just to the right of the entrance.

The exact function of both of these features is not known but they were built at the same time as Newgrange itself, as they were constructed on the original ground level. It seems likely that they were used in the preparation of the dead for burial or religious ceremonies associated with their burial.

A perfectly fitting closing stone (here digitally pictured in position), weighing over a tonne, was used to seal Newgrange when not in use. Its great weight probably meant Newgrange was not used on a day-to-day basis.

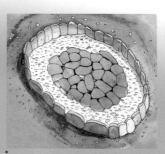

Oval setting

Death, cremation and burial

Cremation was the predominant funeral rite in Ireland in the Neolithic. However, both cremated and uncremated bones have been found at Newgrange. The remains of at least five people, three cremated and two uncremated, were found during the modern excavation. Three hundred years of disturbance, since the rediscovery of Newgrange, has meant that it is impossible to accurately determine the total number of burials or a date for their placement in the chamber.

It is possible that these remains belonged to special people in the community or simply that they were the last people to be buried in the tomb before the demise of the Neolithic culture that built the passage-tombs of Brú na Bóinne. The cremated remains of over 100 individuals have been identified in one recess of the eastern tomb at Knowth, half of whom were juveniles. There is no real way of knowing who had the right to be buried in the tombs of Brú na Bóinne, although the numbers found indicate that the tombs were used for communal burials.

The sequence of events following a death in the community are not known, but it is possible to speculate, based on limited physical evidence. Bodies may have been placed on a platform (or buried) and overtime allowed to disintegrate through natural processes (excarnation). The remains, mostly bone and the grave goods of the person such as beads and pendants, were then cremated. The ash, bone, teeth and artefacts of the dead person were then placed in an urn and brought to the tomb for burial, amid elaborate religious ceremonies, probably close to a significant festival day such as the winter solstice.

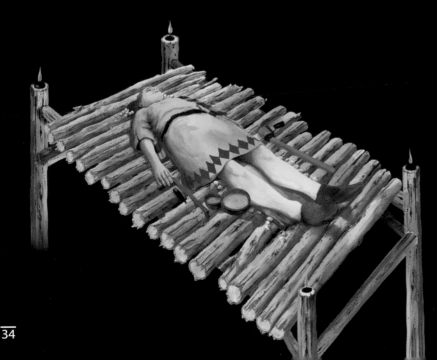

The winter solstice

The winter solstice has always been a major festival in the ancient civilisations of Atlantic Europe. In the pre-Christian world there were practical reasons which made the winter solstice or midwinter a time of plenty and celebration. From this time on, the days became gradually longer, the nights shorter and although the coldest weather was still to come, the spring and warmer weather was not far away. The greatest feast of the year was held at this time, before deep winter set in, because livestock had to be slaughtered, as they could not be fed through the winter. In addition all the autumn harvest had been gathered. This feast eventually became Christmas in the post-pagan world.

It seems likely that the Neolithic people of the Boyne Valley chose this time to bury their loved ones, or at least to temporarily place their cremated remains in the chamber of Newgrange, probably for spiritual reasons associated with the 'rebirth' of the rising sun on the winter solstice.

Some other passage-tombs are orientated to solar events, such as the summer solstice and equinoxes, but the rebirth of the year on the 21st December must have been special, since it probably paralleled the people's religious belief in life, death and then some form of rebirth thereafter. It is easy to imagine a large gathering of people on the morning of the winter solstice, willing the sun to rise to a clear sky, so that it could penetrate the roof-box, light the darkness of the chamber of Newgrange and somehow give new life to their loved ones.

The ceremony probably lasted as long as Neolithic people lived in the Boyne Valley. At some point in the early third millennium (c. 2800BC) Neolithic people were replaced by a new culture. Around the same time, parts of the facade collapsed, burying the roof-box and the entrance. It would be 5,000 years before the sun's rays entered the chamber at Newgrange again.

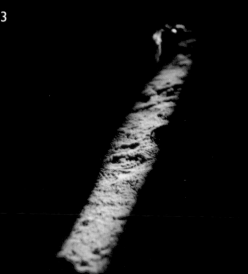

The winter solstice at Newgrange

1) The sun rises over Red Mountain on the south side of the River Boyne at 8:54am (Greenwich Mean Time).

A change in the tilt of the earth over 5,000 years has slightly altered the alignment. In Neolithic times the sun was directly aligned with the roof-box at sunrise. Today this occurs four and a half minutes after sunrise.

2) The sun is directly aligned with the roof-box at 8:58am.

3) A thin beam of golden sunlight enters the chamber, expanding to about 17cm (slightly less than the width of this page). The beam of light, slowly but continuously moves across the floor for 17 minutes, illuminating the chamber before narrowing and then slowly retreating back down the passage. In Neolithic times the beam of sunlight penetrated all the way to the back recess.

4) The beam of sunlight is about as high as it is wide in the chamber.

5) The beam was originally wider, but orthostats at the chamber end of the passage have fallen forward over time (right) and have reduced the width of the beam by as much as 20cm.

The Newgrange Cursus

The Newgrange Cursus is one of the most intriguing monuments of Brú na Bóinne and the one which is least known about and understood. Clearly visible in the field to the east of Newgrange, it has never been excavated as it is situated on privately owned land. The Cursus takes it name from the Latin word for 'course'. Similar structures in England were originally believed to be Roman running tracks and indeed their present day shape somewhat resembles an elongated modern running track.

It is believed that a cursus functioned as a processional avenue and this may also have been the purpose of the Newgrange Cursus, although it could have been used for ceremonial purposes or cremations. The Cursus was built close to the time that Newgrange itself was built.

Regardless of its function, the surviving earthwork is a substantial structure. It is over 35 metres wide and today extends for about 160 metres, but may have been much longer. If this was the case and the Cursus extended for many more metres to the north into the adjoining fields, it would have been the biggest Neolithic structure (by area) in Brú na Bóinne.

Other cursuses may also have existed in Brú na Bóinne, perhaps associated with Knowth and Dowth, but have now been lost. A well preserved cursus that has survived is the 203 metres long 'Banqueting Hall' on the Hill of Tara. Three cursuses, one of three kilometres in length, can also be found close to Stonehenge in England.

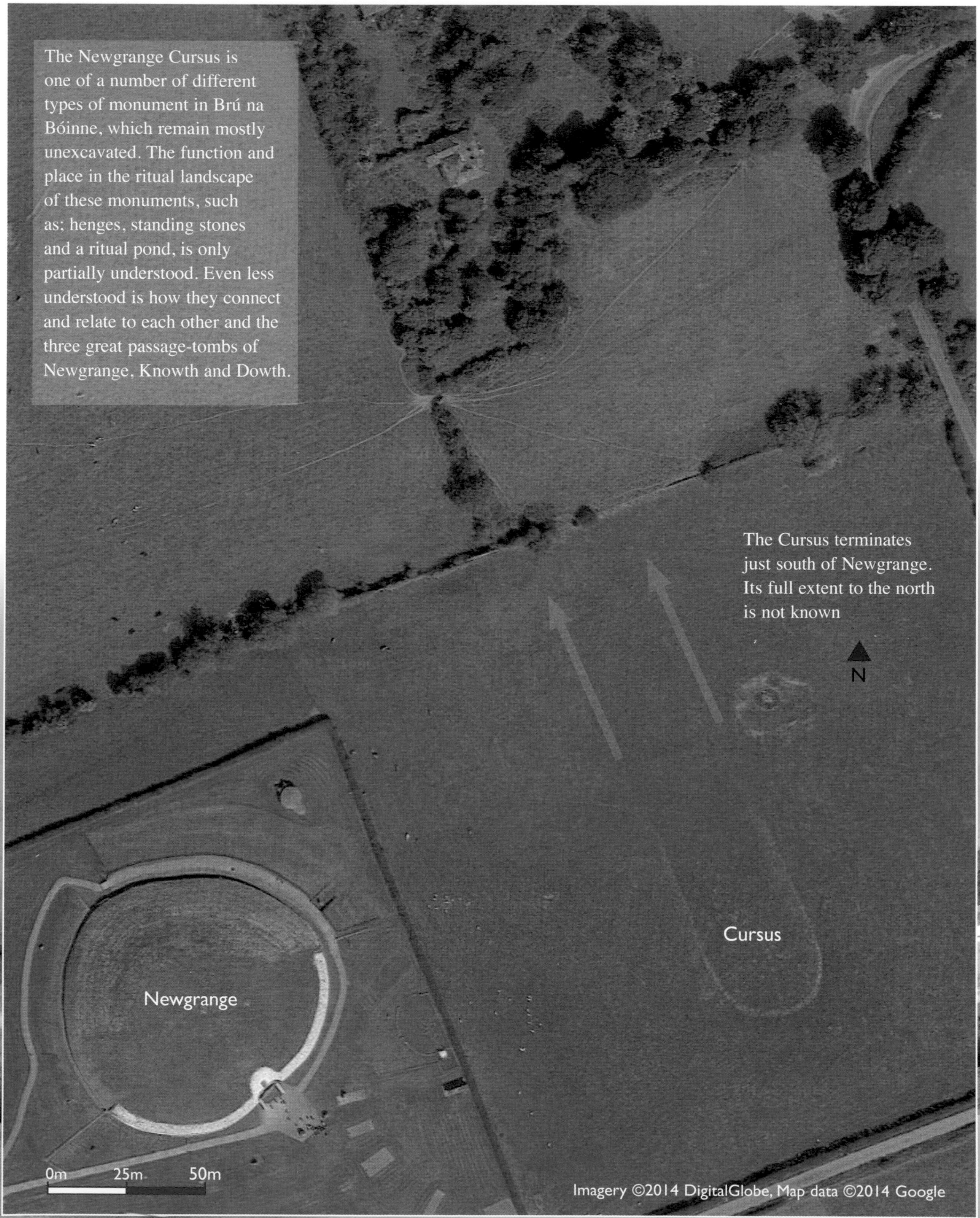

The Newgrange Cursus is one of a number of different types of monument in Brú na Bóinne, which remain mostly unexcavated. The function and place in the ritual landscape of these monuments, such as; henges, standing stones and a ritual pond, is only partially understood. Even less understood is how they connect and relate to each other and the three great passage-tombs of Newgrange, Knowth and Dowth.
The Cursus terminates just south of Newgrange. Its full extent to the north is not known
N
Cursus
Newgrange
0m
25m
50m
Imagery ©2014 DigitalGlobe, Map data ©2014 Google

(left) Conjectural drawing of the Newgrange Cursus at the time of its construction c. 3200BC. The Cursus was probably largely built of earth

There are three smaller 'satellite' passage-tombs within metres of Newgrange and some evidence of a possible fourth. This is a small number compared to the 17 satellites tombs which closely surround Knowth. The smaller satellite tombs resemble Newgrange in many ways and were constructed with a kerb, a passage and a chamber covered by a cairn of stones.

All the satellites tombs have been destroyed down to the level of the first stones. The closest satellite tomb (Z) lies only 23 metres away from Newgrange. All three passage-tombs were excavated in the 1960s.

Directly below Newgrange there are a further two tombs. Both are structurally intact and have never been excavated. Passage-tomb B (below) is the fourth biggest tomb in Brú na Bóinne at 40 metres in diameter.

In ancient times there were at least nine passage-tombs (as well as other monuments) visible from this vantage point on the south side of the Boyne. The view, when travelling on the river, constantly changes as different monuments become more prominent and others recede.

The intact Tomb A is 23 metres in diameter and is just visible here. It is encircled by an earthen henge which has largely been destroyed

Tomb B (foreground) is 40 metres in diameter

West of Newgrange are Site K (20 metres) and L (23 metres) which have largely been destroyed

0m   20m   40m

Newgrange

Z
Z1

Very little of passage-tomb Z remains. Modern concrete blocks mark where the sockets of kerbstones were found

Knowth is situated 1km away, directly behind Newgrange

Newgrange

Passage-tomb Z and a possible tomb Z1 are situated closest to Newgrange

Two passage-tombs, U and E, are situated close to here. They were largely destroyed in previous centuries

Dowth is situated 2km to the northeast and is visible from this point on the Boyne

Newgrange in the Bronze Age

Several hundred years after Newgrange was completed, a new culture replaced the Neolithic builders in the Boyne Valley. Known today as 'Grooved ware' and 'Beaker people' (from their pottery), they recognised Newgrange and Brú na Bóinne as a sacred place and built their own monuments both close to and as part of the ritual complex. It is almost certain that they did not use the chamber for burials as no trace of Beaker artefacts have been found there.

Two huge monuments were built in the Bronze Age as a part of the Newgrange complex; a wooden henge (below) and later, a great stone circle (right) which ringed Newgrange itself. The exact sequence of construction of these monuments is unclear, but the date of construction probably began sometime after 2800BC.

Evidence for the existence of the wooden henge is found only in the soil, the structure having rotted away thousands of years ago. Where there were large wooden posts in the ground, there exists today only a darker coloured soil. Large clay lined pits, containing cremated animal bones were also dug into the ground as part of the henge.

The stone circle is the greatest in Ireland at 105 metres in diameter. Today there are 12 stones still in place and it is estimated that there were originally more than 35. Most of the surviving stones are on the south side of Newgrange close to the entrance.

By 2000BC the Bronze age people were gone and nothing was built at Newgrange for the next 4,000 years.

(right) Four of the stones of the great stone circle which stand near to the entrance of Newgrange

Discovering the wooden henge

(right) Early in the modern excavation of Newgrange, archaeologists discovered an arc of pits and post holes (where wooden posts had been) close to Newgrange. It was believed that the arc extended only for about 30 metres. However, in the 1980s, when archaeologists were excavating close to the road in preparation for the building of visitor facilities, they discovered a similar set of pits and post holes. Was it possible that the existing arc and the new discovery, although 70 metres away, were in some way connected?

Four rectangular areas were excavated at intervals between the two existing discoveries and more pits and post holes were found. A giant circle or wooden henge had been found, approximately the same diameter as the great stone circle which later surrounded Newgrange (105 metres). Above ground it is impossible to know exactly what the wooden henge looked like, but there may have been more to it than simple upright posts. Future excavation may establish the wooden henge to be a much more substantial and sophisticated structure. A second smaller wooden henge monument (20m) was also discovered a short distance to the west of Newgrange.

Although the wooden henge was built within metres of Newgrange and partially blocks the view of Newgrange from the south, it did not block either the entrance or the winter solstice alignment.

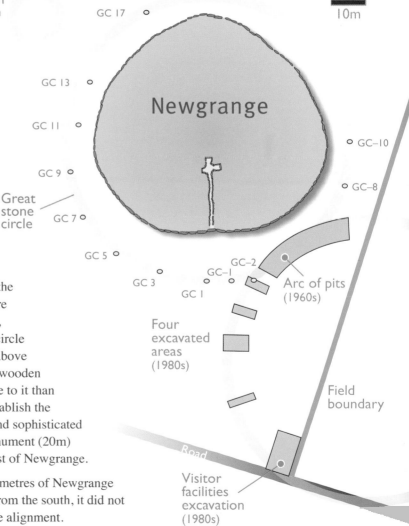

Western wooden henge

GC 17

GC 13

GC 11

Newgrange

GC-10

GC 9

GC-8

Great stone circle

GC 7

10m

GC 5

GC-2

Arc of pits (1960s)

GC 3

GC-1

GC 1

Four excavated areas (1980s)

Field boundary

Road

Visitor facilities excavation (1980s)

Knowth

About 1 kilometre from Newgrange, close to where the bend of the Boyne begins, is the passage-tomb of Knowth. It is in all aspects as great a monument as Newgrange and was probably built around the same time. Their similarities are notable; both occupy high ground within Brú na Bóinne and both are decorated with stone carved art.

There are however, some significant differences. Beneath the mound of Knowth there are two passage-tombs which almost meet in the middle and are separated by only 5 metres of stone.

Cross section through the mound of Knowth

The western passage was the first of Knowth's two tombs to be discovered (1967) during the modern excavation in the 1960s. The kerb curves inwards at this point, which helped identify it as a place where there might be a passage entrance

It is possible to hear the voices of people standing in the other chamber through the 5 metres of rock which separates the two tombs. How this is achieved or whether it has any ritual significance is not known

The western tomb

The narrow western passage and chamber is 34 metres long. It narrows towards its end and is barely wide enough for a person to pass through. It then forms a small undifferentiated chamber (chamber with no recesses) and is just high enough to stand up in.

Monument width
East to West – 80m

Monument length
North to South – 95m

In 1982, this ceremonial mace-head (hammer) was discovered in the excavation of the eastern tomb at Knowth. Its spiral and hollow form a human face, the earliest in Irish Neolithic art. The Knowth mace-head is displayed at the National Museum of Ireland on Dublin's Kildare Street

The mound was constructed using alternating layers of stones and turves. There was a far greater use of turve layers at Knowth than at Newgrange

This small satellite tomb (Site 16) was built before Knowth and modified when the much larger main tomb was built beside it

The eastern passage is orientated towards the rising sun on the morning of the equinox (March 21st and September 22nd), when the length of the day is as long as the night. The western passage is aligned to sunset on the same days

Ditches cut into the mound behind the kerb during the Early Christian period (see p.51), destroyed the original entrances to both passages for a distance of about 4 metres. This destruction means the sun's rays can no longer penetrate the passage of both tombs

The long eastern passage

The eastern tomb

The eastern tomb consists of a passage and a cruciform chamber with three recesses. Its combined length is 40 metres.

Dowth

Dowth is the third great passage tomb of Brú na Bóinne. It is similar in many ways to Newgrange and Knowth, equally as big and also positioned on high ground above the River Boyne. Differences occur only in the scale and positioning of the passages and chambers. Dowth's two known passages are much shorter, close to each other and have been open for centuries. The setting sun on the evening of the winter solstice illuminates the south chamber of Dowth.

Kerbstones

A kerb of an estimated 115 stones surrounds the base of the mound of Dowth. Only one stone is known to have substantial carvings, the 'Stone of the Seven Suns' (below). Many of the kerbstones remain buried

Dowth today

South chamber

North chamber

Souterrain

Modern entrance

Dowth's great hollow

The great passage-tomb of Dowth survived virtually intact for 5,000 years, until the mid-19th century. An amateur archaeologist, who favoured instant results over slow and painstaking work, began to dig at Dowth. Frustrated at the lack of progress and keen to find any treasure that might be buried, he placed a quantity of explosives in the centre of the cairn. The explosion blew a huge crater in the cairn, burst his eardrums, but resulted in not a single piece of treasure.

Chambers

The two burial chambers in the mound are within 25 metres of one another. The passages are shorter than those found at Newgrange and Knowth, but the chambers are as large.

In the late Iron Age (c. 400AD) a souterrain was built by people living in and around Dowth, which shared an entrance with the northern passage. A souterrain is an underground stone-lined chamber built for the storage of goods and for the safety of people if under attack.

Comparisons

The chamber at Newgrange bears a striking similarity to the eastern chamber of its near neighbour, Knowth (in plan on right).

Both have:

▮ cruciform chambers with three smaller recesses

▮ long passages, though the eastern passage and chamber at Knowth (40m) is much longer than that at Newgrange (24m)

▮ curves incorporated into their passages. At Newgrange the curves serve to reduce the amount of indirect sunlight entering the chamber.

It seems likely, given the proximity and the similarity of the design of Newgrange and Knowth, that they were built within a short time of each other. To build one chamber of such complexity was a towering achievement. To repeat the process reaffirms the incredible skill, commmitment and ambition of the builders of Brú na Bóinne.

The seemingly erratic symmetrical layout of Newgrange's chamber looks more deliberate when compared with Knowth's eastern chamber.

Neither chamber is truly symmetrical, but both chambers follow the same deviations, the right recess being slightly higher than the left recess.

The right recess is the largest recess and is semi-enclosed. It also houses the most elaborate basin stone.

0m

5m

Newgrange   **Knowth**

Path of sunlight at sunrise on the winter solstice, 21st December

Possible path of sunlight around the time of the spring (22nd March) and autumn equinox (22nd September) at sunrise

The three great monuments of Brú na Bóinne – Newgrange, Knowth and Dowth – in plan, comparing orientation and the scale of the passages and chambers

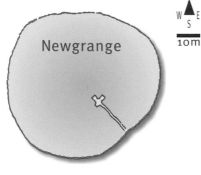

Newgrange

N
W E
S

10m

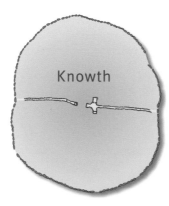

Knowth

Dowth

Pilgrimage

hree and a half thousand years after Newgrange was built, a group of people, living in ancient but historic times, gathered close to the monument's buried entrance stone. They dug a hole and placed a small but valuable offering inside. Numerous Roman coins, two ancient gold torques, two gold rings and a gold chain constitute the most valuable hoard of Roman artefacts ever found in Ireland.

Was the hoard an offering from a Roman official on a diplomatic mission to Tara, the seat of the High Kings of Ireland (20km away), perhaps seeking an end to raiding by Irish tribes on the faltering Roman colony of Britannia? Or was it an offering from a native Irish chief, who, having successfully raided the Romano-British coast (only 100km away), chose to give thanks to the gods of his ancestors by leaving part of the haul at Newgrange?

Whatever the reason, it is clear that 3,500 years after it was built, Newgrange still maintained a spiritual draw for people, who felt compelled to leave votive offerings. Newgrange had always been a place of pilgrimage in the Neolithic and Bronze Age world, but this hoard and many others tell us that despite the fact that it was no longer in use, Newgrange remained an important spiritual centre for people on the island and beyond, ranging over thousands of years.

Another sign of its continued importance was that Newgrange was never built upon, despite its strategic position on the River Boyne, unlike Knowth and Dowth, which both saw centuries of occupation and a variety of uses by many different cultures.

A generation after the Roman hoard was deposited in the ground, the religious landscape of the country was to change for ever. St Patrick arrived in Ireland from the west coast of Britain and elected to begin his Christian mission on the Hill of Slane only 4 kilometres from Brú na Bóinne, probably recognising that the area was the key to the spiritual heartland of Ireland. Despite the adoption of the new Christian

A hole is dug for the burial of a votive offering at Newgrange at some time in the late 4th century AD. It seems likely that if a Roman diplomatic delegation came the short distance across the Irish Sea, they would have been accompanied by an impressive show of force

(Left to right) Four Roman emperors of the 4th cenury AD,
Maximian (286 – 305AD), Constantine II (317 – 340AD), Gratian (367 – 383AD), Arcadius (383 – 408AD),
adorn some of the coins from the hoard found close to the entrance of Newgrange

religion, Brú na Bóinne continued to be recognised as a sacred place. It is mentioned in many mediaeval books, including the 12th century *Senchas na Relec* (*The History of the Cemeteries*), which was part of the *Lebor na hUidre* (*Book of the Dun Cow*), as one of the most important burial places of Ireland.

Today many people travel from all over the world to Brú na Bóinne for spiritual reasons, seeking communion with their ancient ancestors and their way of life, making Newgrange the oldest pilgrimage destination in the world in more or less continuous use.

(above) Knowth was converted in the later Iron Age (c. 350AD) into a ringfort and stronghold in the Kingdom of North Brega. Two deep concentric ditches were dug into the mound as a defence, damaging the passage-tomb in the process

Newgrange vandalised

It is perhaps fortunate that the facade of Newgrange collapsed after its Neolithic builders were gone, burying the entrance and thereby keeping people out of the chamber for the greatest part of its existence. Ironically, the collapse (of the quartz wall) may itself have been the first act of vandalism at Newgrange, by Bronze Age people who lived close to the monument. Both Knowth and Dowth were also used by many other cultures at different times, as both dwelling places and fortresses, which unfortunately resulted in the removal of huge amounts of stone. Newgrange, since the end of the Bronze Age occupation, has remained largely untouched, until its re-discovery in 1699.

Within years of its re-discovery, visitors were removing anything that could be carried from the chamber. An intriguing 'pyramidal-shaped' stone, recorded in the 18th century as being in the centre of the chamber, disappeared and has not been seen since. The removal of stones from the cairn itself also began to take its toll on Newgrange.

In 1797, a man from Connaught had a dream that there was treasure under the basin stone in the northern recess at Newgrange. Unrestricted access allowed this deluded individual to dig a large hole under it, thereby breaking the stone into six pieces. He went home empty-handed, with no treasure, but irreparable damage was done to that part of the chamber and any

possible archaeological information contained therein.

Unfortunately the vandalism continued unabated into the 19th century. Many others, described by one concerned writer as 'evilly-disposed visitors', left their names (below left) and the date of their visit carved into the stones of the chamber and passage.

By the middle of the 19th century, scholars and antiquarians such as Sir William Wilde (father of Oscar Wilde) were drawn to Newgrange, due in part to a growing awareness of Ireland's ancient past. William Wilde's book, *The Beauties of the Boyne and its tributary, the Blackwater*, described in detail, for the first time, the recently revealed entrance stone and the roof-box lintel.

In 1882, as a result of the growing awareness and a concern about the continuous damage being done to Newgrange, the three great tombs of Brú na Bóinne were listed as National Monuments. Crucially, a gate was installed at the entrance to the passage of Newgrange to stop people visiting without supervision. The 20th century saw the first unofficial guide service to Newgrange. This was eventually replaced in 1980 by a state-run full-time guide service, whose mission continues to be to protect and preserve the monument for future generations.

Artefacts

For such a huge monument, built over many decades and in use for more than 1,000 years by both Neolithic and Bronze Age people, Newgrange has thrown up surprisingly few artefacts of significance from these times. There were however many everyday objects, such as the small lamp, thousands of flint implements, shards of broken pottery, animal bones and bone objects found at the site. In the chamber of Newgrange (disturbed for over 300 years) were small grave goods such as pendants, beads and human bone.

(left) A part of a stone macehead or hammer head found near Newgrange

(right) This bronze axe was found, during the modern excavation, close to kerbstone 81. It is one of the earliest bronze axes found in Ireland and could have been manufactured in a metal working area that existed at Newgrange in the early Bronze Age. Its presence at Newgrange marks the end of 1,000 years of Neolithic culture in Brú na Bóinne

(above) Three of the many thousands of worked flint artefacts found at Newgrange during the modern excavation

(below) This lamp is one of three found at Newgrange. It is made of granite and was found near the entrance to Newgrange. A small piece of fur or twine served as a wick, which floated in animal fat. Many of the Newgrange artefacts are on display (or stored) in the National Museum of Ireland on Dublin's Kildare Street

(left) A phallus-like object shaped from sandstone and measuring 240mm by 75mm (pictured half size here) was found close to the entrance of Newgrange in the oval setting feature (p.34). Although Newgrange itself is often considered to be representative of the female gender, there are many artefacts found in Brú na Bóinne, such as this stone, which are representative of the male gender.

Comparisons can be made with this stone and larger standing stones, such as the 'Lia Fáil' (The stone of Destiny) on the Hill of Tara, 20km away (right). There are also many examples of standing stones in Europe which match the dimensions of this artefact, albeit many times bigger

Newgrange excavated

On a cold November morning in 1961 a small group of archaeologists gathered outside the entrance of Newgrange. They were the leaders in the field of this relatively undeveloped science in Ireland and the meeting proved to be amongst the most important gatherings at any prehistoric Irish site in modern times.

The archaeologists had gathered to decide on what to do with the monument. Its fame was growing steadily and it was now open all year round to an increasing number of visitors. It had been repaired several times since it had come into state care in 1882, but by 1960 Newgrange looked neglected and in places was dangerous.

The archaeologists, amongst them Professor Michael O'Kelly (right), discussed a possible course of action and decided that Newgrange must first be excavated (for the first time on a large scale), before it could be restored and made safe for visitors. O'Kelly was one of the leading archaeologists in Ireland, an expert in excavation and Professor of Archaeology at University College Cork. He had spent the previous three decades excavating sites in Ireland on a practical and experimental level, but believed that this particular excavation would prove to be 'rather dull' and a couple of summer seasons would finish the necessary work.

Digging started at Newgrange in the summer of 1962 and after two summers of work it became clear to O'Kelly and his team that what lay beneath the ground would require a full excavation on a scale never before seen in Ireland. The aim of the excavation now became to discover as much as possible about Newgrange and to attempt to answer many of the questions that such a large and impressive monument asked. O'Kelly would also examine the evidence in an attempt to discover what Newgrange looked like when it was first built. This would assist in the conservation and restoration of Newgrange.

To prepare for their work on Newgrange, O'Kelly and his team travelled to places such as Brittany, Spain and Portugal to study European passage-tombs and to draw comparisons between them and Newgrange. O'Kelly also consulted with the leading experts in other countries on the various features found at Newgrange and brought in experts in different areas from Ireland to advise on the restoration of the great cairn of stones which had collapsed outwards.

First steps

Before excavation could begin, the trees and shrubs which were causing so much damage to the monument were cleared. Surveys were carried out on the cairn and the ridge on which it stood, as well as the interior of the tomb and the visible art of Newgrange.

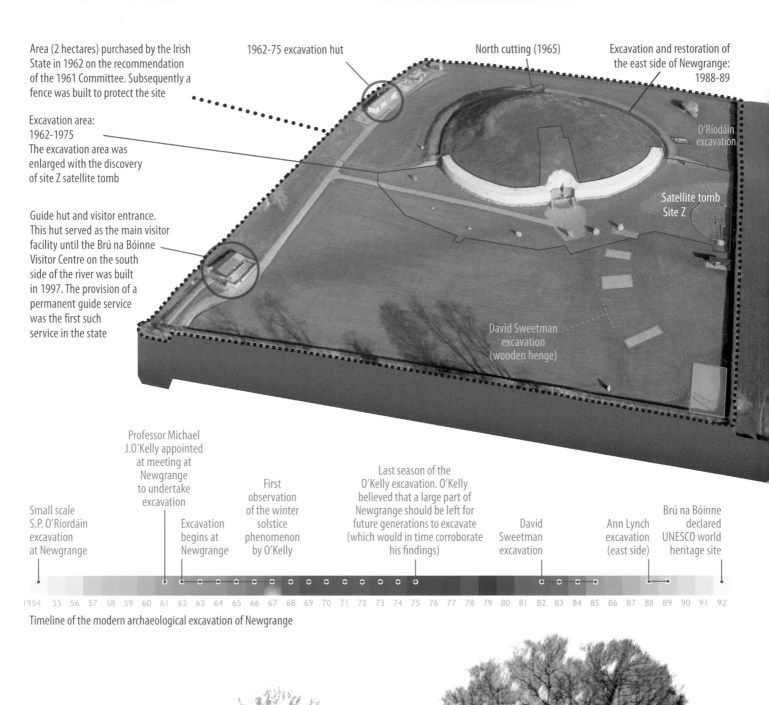

Area (2 hectares) purchased by the Irish State in 1962 on the recommendation of the 1961 Committee. Subsequently a fence was built to protect the site

1962-75 excavation hut

North cutting (1965)

Excavation and restoration of the east side of Newgrange: 1988-89

O'Ríodáin excavation

Excavation area: 1962-1975 The excavation area was enlarged with the discovery of site Z satellite tomb

Satellite tomb Site Z

Guide hut and visitor entrance. This hut served as the main visitor facility until the Brú na Bóinne Visitor Centre on the south side of the river was built in 1997. The provision of a permanent guide service was the first such service in the state

David Sweetman excavation (wooden henge)

Small scale S.P. O'Ríordáin excavation at Newgrange

Professor Michael J.O'Kelly appointed at meeting at Newgrange to undertake excavation

Excavation begins at Newgrange

First observation of the winter solstice phenomenon by O'Kelly

Last season of the O'Kelly excavation. O'Kelly believed that a large part of Newgrange should be left for future generations to excavate (which would in time corroborate his findings)

David Sweetman excavation

Ann Lynch excavation (east side)

Brú na Bóinne declared UNESCO world heritage site

1954 55 56 57 58 59 60 61 62 63 64 65 66 67 68 69 70 71 72 73 74 75 76 77 78 79 80 81 82 83 84 85 86 87 88 89 90 91 92

Timeline of the modern archaeological excavation of Newgrange

(left) Newgrange before the excavation began in 1962. Known affectionately as the 'candlelight days', the chamber was visited with the aid of candle light.

Excavating the slip

Professor O'Kelly began the excavation close to the entrance area of the cairn (below), as it was here that repairs and conservation were needed urgently. A smaller excavation at the back of the cairn was also carried out. Over the course of 13 years of excavation, much of what had previously been believed about the structure of Newgrange was proved to be incorrect. O'Kelly introduced new methods and new science to Irish archaeology during the excavation, such as the recently invented radiocarbon dating method. The age of Newgrange was pushed back another 1,700 years, with a 95% certainty that the passage-tomb was constructed sometime between 3,370BC and 2,920BC. He also had samples of pollen and the humble snail shell analysed, which provided clues as to what the environment looked like when Newgrange was built.

Two members of the excavation team record the profile of the slip at Kerbstone 4. Amongst the most important aspects of the modern excavation was the accurate recording of what was found in the slip as it was exposed. Prof O'Kelly had abandoned engineering and architecture in favour of archaeology whilst a student, but had retained an appreciation of accurate surveying and record keeping.

Detail of Survey drawing at K96 (O'Kelly Archive, NMS)

19th century ditch and retaining wall

Slip
(Stones from the cairn which have collapsed forward in ancient times)

Electricity was installed in the chamber at Newgrange in 1957. Here the cable is re-exposed by the excavation.

Excavation has exposed several hearths belonging to the substantial Bronze Age occupation of the site.

The Oval setting feature has been completely excavated.

Professor O'Kelly (bottom), Claire O'Kelly and W.P. le Clerc of National Monuments discuss an aspect of the excavation.

An archaeologist excavates the quartz/granite layer found above the original ground level (see p.57).

At this early stage of the excavation (1965 – season 3) some of the area in front of the entrance has been excavated to the original ground level and the slip is being excavated in sections.

The roof-box and part of the passage has been exposed by removing some of the cairn. The aperture of the roof-box was blocked, leading O'Kelly to describe it as a 'box' where offerings could be left. It would be another two years before the purpose of this unique feature was properly established.

(right) Only the carved lintel of the roof-box was visible before O'Kelly's excavation

Roof-box

Entrance stone

Kerbstone 96

Newgrange
(in plan)

This view represents approximately 4% of the mound

The facade

The facade, or exterior wall, is without question the most controversial feature of Newgrange in modern times. It was, for a distance of some 60 metres on either side of the entrance, entirely reconstructed in the 1970s under Professor O'Kelly's supervision, using the white quartz and granite-rolled boulders excavated from the slip. In 1961 before the excavation of Newgrange had begun, it was planned that all the material of the slip would be placed back on the cairn, which would then form a hemispherical shape. O'Kelly's findings changed everything and left him with an enormous dilemma.

The layer of white quartz and granite was too substantial to be anything other than an important part of the monument. It lay in a continuous layer on the original ground level, 0.5m at its thickest and as far from the kerb as 8 metres. The quartz could have been a path still in its original position or it could have formed some part of the facade of Newgrange.

O'Kelly was convinced from the evidence he uncovered, of the latter. He found that in all cases where a kerbstone had fallen forward, and many had, there was no quartz found beneath it (see diagram right). Other original Neolithic features, such as the oval setting (p.33), were completely covered by the layer of quartz. He believed this layer must have fallen from above the kerb and had formed a near vertical wall in ancient times.

O'Kelly conducted a practical experiment to test his theory. Using some of the original quartz, he built a wall above a part of the kerb. He then collapsed it to see how it would form on the ground. The resulting deposition was 'well-nigh identical' to what he had found in his excavation of the slip. He concluded from the amount of stone in the slip, that the wall had been about 3 metres high above the kerb and controversially, was at a steep angle of about 10 degrees off the vertical.

Whether or not Professor O'Kelly got it right will be forever debated. What is certain is that, while Newgrange was in use in Neolithic times, the white quartz and granite boulder were meant to stand out in the green of the countryside and proclaim to all who viewed it, that Newgrange was a building separate from the hill on which it stood and most importantly for the prestige of its builders, was one of the great buildings of their age. This is the function it still performs today.

The stones of the kerb were carefully positioned by the builders, so that the top side formed an even line and there was a flat surface on which the quartz wall could be built

This diagram represents Professor O'Kelly's case for a near vertical quartz/granite wall. He believed that the outer cairn collapsed at three different times to create the slip which buried the kerb and entrance of Newgrange:

1) The quartz/granite facade, which was built on the kerbstones, collapsed forward in a 'fairly rapid and clean collapse'

2) A second collapse occurred, this time it was the material of the cairn pushing outwards. A considerable time elapsed before the next collapse as vegetation and soil had built up

3) A third collapse occurred possibly as a result of an earth tremor, resulting in a great slide of stones from the cairn. The slip merged with the cairn, disguising Newgrange as part of the hill on which it stood.

(right) A profile of the slip close to the entrance of Newgrange in 1962, during the modern excavation. This section at kerbstone 96 reveals the material of the three collapses. O'Kelly recognised that it was easier to interpret the slip from its profile rather than from above.

It has been suggested that the quartz wall was deliberately pulled down once the original Neolithic builders had gone, in an act of slighting the monument. This might account for the 'clean collapse' which O'Kelly found on the ground level.

(below) The reconstructed facade today.
A white facade has been the choice of many builders of monumental buildings in history: the pyramids of Giza (a white limestone layer originally covered the pyramids), the Neolithic long barrows of Southern England (faced in chalk), the Parthenon of Athens (white marble) and Cairn T, a passage-tomb in Lough Crew, 50km from Brú na Bóinne (white quartz)

The winter solstice of 1967

Over the course of the modern excavation, some of the many local visitors would often tell Professor O'Kelly of a tradition, that the rising sun at some unspecified time, would light up the triple-spiral stone in the end recess of the chamber at Newgrange. Unfortunately, according to Prof O'Kelly, "no one could be found who had witnessed this but it continued to be mentioned" over and over again. O'Kelly at first assumed that there was a confusion with Stonehenge and the well-known midsummer sunrise alignment there.

Discussions between Prof O'Kelly and his wife Claire, on the persistence of this tradition, planted in their minds the idea that "a southeast orientation would be correct at the midwinter solstice" and that perhaps this was more than a figment of the local people's slightly confused collective imaginations.

Abandoning the preparations for Christmas to Claire, Prof O'Kelly made the long journey from Cork to Newgrange a few days before the winter solstice, the shortest day of the year, to test out this hunch.

Rising in darkness on the 21st December, Prof O'Kelly pulled back the curtains of his hotel room to reveal a star-filled, cloudless sky. He drove the short distance to Newgrange and walked quietly towards the tomb.

Some minutes before sunrise, Prof O'Kelly stood alone in the darkness of the chamber at Newgrange, wondering what, if anything, would happen.

To his amazement a thin beam of golden sunlight pierced the darkness of the chamber and minute by minute grew steadily wider and brighter, "lighting up everything as it came, until the whole chamber – side recesses, floor and roof six metres above the floor – were all clearly illuminated". Prof O'Kelly stood transfixed by the phenomenon, fearful in his own imagination that the Dagda, the great pagan god, might punish him by hurling the roof down upon him.

Fortunately the roof remained in place, the sun slowly retreated and he walked from the tomb into the morning sunlight, the first person for 5,000 years to have witnessed the light of the mid-winter sun penetrate the darkness of the chamber at Newgrange.

Subsequent investigation by Dr Jon Patrick, commissioned by Prof O'Kelly, established that the orientation of Newgrange towards the rising sun of the winter solstice was deliberate. Patrick reported that, "It therefore seems that the sun [if not blocked] has shone into the chamber ever since the day of its construction and will probably continue to do so for ever". Further observation by Prof O'Kelly established that the spectacle occurs for a short number of days before and after the winter solstice. He himself would witness it at least once a year for the remainder of his life.

Since the discovery of the winter solstice phenomenon at Newgrange, archaeologists have gone on to discover other solar alignments of megalithic monuments in Ireland and elsewhere.

Brú na Bóinne today

oday Brú na Bóinne is in the care of the Irish State, which provides visitor facilities and ensures that the wonders of the Boyne Valley are protected for future generations. In 1993, Brú na Bóinne was declared a World Heritage Site by UNESCO. Newgrange and Brú na Bóinne can be visited every day of the year, except four days around Christmas day.

The winter solstice is observed every 21st of December by a small group of people, lucky enough to have won a place in the chamber through a public lottery. If their luck holds and the sky is clear just above the horizon line on the other side of the valley from Newgrange, they will share with the ancient people of Brú na Bóinne, one of the oldest celebrations humanity has devised.

The land within Brú na Bóinne is still farmed today, over 6,000 years after the first farmers began to farm the area in the Neolithic. It remains one of the most beautiful, fertile and fascinating places on earth.

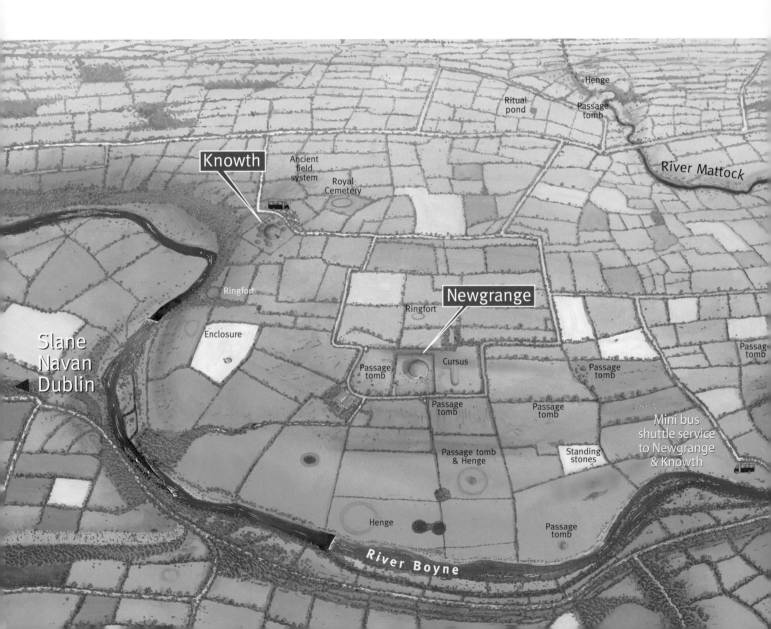

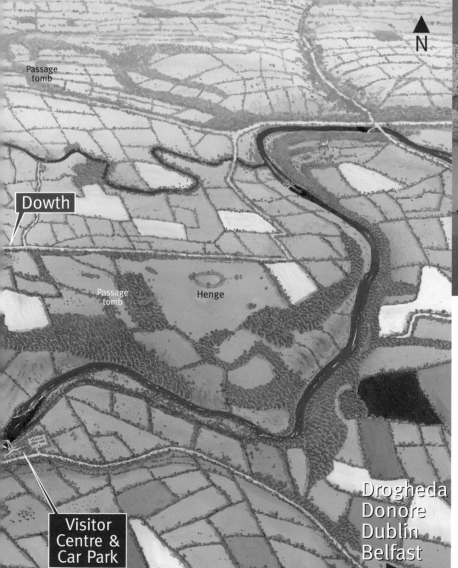

Passage tomb

Dowth

Passage tomb

Henge

Visitor Centre & Car Park

Drogheda
Donore
Dublin
Belfast

N

(clockwise from left) The World Heritage Site of Brú na Bóinne

Sunrise over Red Mountain on the morning of the winter solstice

People gathering on the 19th December to observe the winter solstice phenomenon. The aperture of the roof-box is wide enough for the rising sun to enter the chamber of Newgrange two days either side of the 21st December

Newgrange in the snow

(above) A view of Newgrange from the south side of the River Boyne on Red Mountain. It is from this position that the sun rises on the morning of the winter solstice.

To the left of Newgrange, in the near distance is the grassy mound of Knowth, situated 1km away

(left) Newgrange from the west. The monument sits on the highest point of this part of Brú na Bóinne. In the distance is land on the south side of the River Boyne

(below) The entrance stone (K1). The grey limestone wall behind K1 was used to make a wider entrance and exit area in the 1960/70s reconstruction. The original entrance was much narrower, with the entrance stone forming a barrier. The grey limestone wall was designed to be deliberately different from the quartz wall